A Kid's
Best Friend

Maya Ajmera and Alex Fisher

with a foreword by Super Gus of Planet Dog

SHAKTI for *Children*

Rrrrr…Hi!

Wanna Run?

Wanna Catch?

Wanna Play?

My name's Gus, but call me Super Gus. I live in a place called Planet Dog—a place full of kids and dogs, friendship and fun, where flowers smell good, the grass is green, the sky is blue, and tails are always wagging. On Planet Dog and around the world, dogs, like kids, come in every shape, size, and color. Dogs can be big or small, have short tails or long tails. Dogs can have different color eyes, tongues, noses, or even spots or stripes.

And just like kids, it makes no difference what a dog looks like, or where it lives. No matter what, kids and dogs can be respectful, loyal, and loving toward one another. The relationship you share with your dog is like no other. After all, a dog is a kid's best friend.

 Woof,
Super Gus

New Zealand

Bhutan

Russia

A kid's

United States

Indonesia

best friend

Canada

is a dog

with big floppy ears,

United States

United States

a wagging tail,

and a wet nose...

...with a big tongue
and sloppy kisses

to lick
and tickle
your face
clean.

United States

A dog is a best friend

Colombia

India

for playing,

and rolling,

United States

and

running

like the

wind.

Nigeria

A friend for

Poland

Argentina

getting

United States

messy, and clean.

United States

A friend for

United States

Canada

cuddling and feeding

and caring

Bulgaria

Mexico

 Canada

 United States

for each other

on
cold
mornings
and

Peru

Ecuador

United States

Benin

hot
afternoons.

And when the
day is over,
shut your eyes
with your best friend,
be a pillow,
and snuggle into
deep sleep.

A dog is

a kid's

Australia

best friend.

All Kinds of Dogs

Just like people, no two dogs are the same. Some are big, while others are small, with long tails or short tails. Dogs can have stripes or spots. Their fur can be curly, shaggy, silky, spiky, long, or short. There are many different breeds, such as Chihuahua, a tiny dog originally from Mexico; Border Collie, from Australia; or Newfoundland, a huge dog from Canada. Many dogs are mutts: a combination of different breeds.

Having Fun

Dogs love to learn tricks. You can teach a dog to sit, play dead, roll over, shake hands, crawl, and even high-five. Dogs enjoy water. They jump and swim in rivers, ponds, and ocean waves. You may love to roll around in the grass or run around in your backyard with your dog. Like you, dogs love toys, especially squeaky ones that make noise. Dogs enjoy catching sticks, tennis balls, and Frisbees. Dogs know how to have fun!

Special Care

Dogs are faithful friends, but they do need care. They have to be fed well and given water. Dogs love juicy bones and dog biscuits. Washing and scrubbing your dog is vital to its health. Their hair must be brushed and sometimes cut when it gets too long. Exercise is also important. Dogs can't go all day without exercise. You have to take your dog outside to walk and run and play.

Ways Dogs Serve

Dogs are important. They can protect you from harm by barking at strangers. They can serve as police dogs that help the police sniff out danger. Guide dogs help blind people live active lives. Because of their intelligence, strength, and keen sense of smell, some dogs are rescue dogs. Certain types of dogs help pull fishing nets or haul wood. All over the world, they help look after farm animals like sheep or goats. Dogs are an important part of your family and your community.

Your Best Friend

Your dog gives you unconditional love. In the morning, your dog jumps onto your bed to wake you. When you get home from school, your dog is waiting with a wagging tail, ready to make you happy. Like all best friends, dogs can sense your feelings. They know how to cheer you up when you are sick or sad by snuggling into bed with you or licking your face with loads of kisses. Your dog is your very best friend.

To my two 'best friends' Seeger and Murphy. . . woof—Alex

Special woofs to all the dogs at Planet Dog and Planet Dog Philanthropy for their generosity and support. To Maya, thanks for taking me on the journey and showing me the way, and to Jen for being there all along. Wag—Alex Fisher

My thanks to Alex for his creativity and friendship!—Maya Ajmera

Our heartfelt gratitude to Melany Kuhn for her superb design for *A Kid's Best Friend*. In addition, our thanks to Lindsey Heard-Maloney of Planet Dog Philanthropy and Stuart Maloney of Planet Dog for their enthusiastic support of this project. We would also like to thank our families.

Our thanks to all the photographers who participated in this project. Without the photographs, there would be no book. Many thanks to Peter Rapalus at Canine Companions for his support of this project.

A Kid's Best Friend is a project of Shakti for Children and Planet Dog Philanthropy. Financial support for this project has been provided by the Flora Family Foundation, Planet Dog, Inc., and the W.K. Kellogg Foundation.

SHAKTI FOR CHILDREN is dedicated to teaching children to value diversity and to grow into productive and caring citizens of the world. It is a program of the Global Fund for Children, a non-profit organization, committed to advancing the human rights of children and youth.Visit www.globalfundforchildren.org
PLANET DOG PHILANTHROPY is dedicated to supporting unique and effective programs taking compassionate action to preserve and restore the natural environment, cultivate animal welfare, and foster quality education. Visit www.planetdogphilanthropy.org

Published by Charlesbridge Publishing
85 Main Street, Watertown, MA 02472
(617) 926-0329 • www. charlesbridge.com

Developed by Shakti for Children/The Global Fund for Children
1612 K Street, NW Suite 706 Washington, DC 20006
(202) 331-9003 • www.shakti.org

Details about donation of royalties can be obtained by writing Charlesbridge Publishing, Planet Dog Philanthropy, and the Global Fund for Children.

To Elena and Lidia and their best friend, Beijo—Maya

Library of Congress Cataloging-in-Publication Data
Ajmera, Maya.
A kid's best friend / Maya Ajmera and Alex Fisher.
    p.   cm. — (It's a kid's world)
Summary: Describes the special relationship that exists between children and their pet dogs all around the world.
    ISBN 1-57091-513-X (reinforced for library use)
    ISBN 1-57091-514-8 (softcover)
1. Dogs—Juvenile literature. 2. Dogs—Social aspects—Juvenile literature. 3. Children and animals—Juvenile literature.
4. Human-animal relationships—Juvenile literature. [1. Dogs.
2. Pets. 3. Human-animal relationships.] I. Fisher, Alex. II. Title.
III. Series.
SF426.5.A42   2002
636.7'0887—dc21   2001005933

Printed in South Korea
(hc)   10 9 8 7 6 5 4 3 2 1
(sc)   10 9 8 7 6 5 4 3 2 1

Photographs: (left to right and top to bottom): Cover: © 1997 Margaret Miller/Photo Researchers; Title Page: © Jeffrey Dunn, © Victor Englebert, © Nik Wheeler, © John Russell/Network Aspen, © Eastcott/Momatiuk/Woodfin Camp, © Victor Englebert; p.2: © Planet Dog, Inc.; p.3: Arthus Bertrand/Jacana/Photo Researchers; p. 4: © 2001 Jon Warren, © B & C Alexander/Photo Researchers; pp. 4-5: © Victor Englebert; p.5: © Jeffrey Dunn; p.6: © Eastcott/Momatiuk/Woodfin Camp; p. 7: © Porterfield /Chickering/Photo Researchers; p.8: © Nik Wheeler; pp.8-9: © Catherine Ursillo/Photo Researchers; p.9: © Eastcott/Momatiuk /Woodfin Camp; pp. 10-11: © M. Schwarz/Image Works; p. 12: © Victor Englebert, © Dinodia Picture Agency; p.13: © Carolyn A. McKeone/Photo Researchers; p.14; © John Russell/Network Aspen; p.15; © 2000 Jon Warren; p. 16: © Eastcott/Momatiuk /Photo Researchers; pp. 16-17: © Victor Englebert; p. 17: © John Russell/Network Aspen; p.18: © Jeffrey Dunn; p.19: © Jeffrey Dunn, © Eastcott/Momatiuk/Woodfin Camp; p.20: © 2000 Jon Warren, © Dana Hyde/Photo Researchers; p.21: © Momatiuk/ Eastcott/Woodfin Camp, © Canine Companions; pp.22-23: Ulrike Welsch/Photo Researchers; p. 24: © Victor Englebert, © Victor Englebert, © John Russell/Network Aspen; p. 25: © Victor Englebert; pp.26-27: ©Monkmeyer/Conklin; p.28: © Camille Tokerud/Photo Researchers; p.29: © Bill Bachman/Photo Researchers; p.30: © Porterfield/Chickering/Photo Researchers, © 2000 Jon Warren, © Eastcott/Momatiuk/Woodfin Camp; p. 31: © Victor Englebert, © Jeffrey Dunn; Back cover: © Jeffrey Dunn, © Victor Englebert, © Nik Wheeler, © John Russell/Network Aspen, © Eastcott/Momatiuk/Woodfin Camp, © Victor Englebert.